A-MAZE-ING
NATURAL
PHENOMENA

written by Eryl Nash

illustrated by Sarah Dennis

IN THIS BOOK

Nature is a powerful force that nourishes and brings life to our planet. From the tiniest grain of sand to the enormous expanse of sky above us, it is everywhere we look. Nature has the power to dazzle us. From the breathtaking beauty of glow-in-the-dark ocean waves to the sheer power of ferocious supercell storms, there are some phenomena on Earth that have to be seen to be believed.

In this book you can read all about these incredible natural phenomena:

Northern Lights

page 16

Bioluminescent Waves

page 20

Waterfall Rainbows

page 24

Volcanic Eruptions

page 28

There is a scientific explanation for each of these phenomena. Turn to the relevant pages to find out how they happen and see each natural wonder come to life. Take your time and see what you can discover!

Can you make your way through the mazes and spot the hidden items as you go?

MACKEREL SKIES

The air around us contains lots of invisible water in the form of a gas called vapour. Warm air can hold lots of this vapour but, as air rises, it cools and the vapour turns into tiny water droplets. The droplets emerge from the vapour, then join together with particles of salt and dust. These all stick together to make the cloud formations we can see in the sky. Mackerel skies are named for the clouds looking like a pattern on a mackerel's back. *'Mackerel sky, mackerel sky, never long wet, never long dry'* is a saying that tells the cloud formation predicts wet or stormy weather ahead.

How does this phenomenon happen?

1 When a stormy front of warm air meets a clear front of cold air, the less dense warm air gently rises above the heavy cold air.

2 As the warm air rises, the water vapour turns straight into ice crystals because of the low temperatures at this high altitude.

3 The ice crystals form a very thin layer of wispy clouds that cover a large area. These are high-level 'cirrus' clouds.

4 Ripples form in the layer as the cold air pushes back against the warm air that moves across it. This gives the effect of the scales on a mackerel's skin.

A Sunset Maze

Sunset spreads across a mackerel sky, signalling to the fishermen of this sleepy Welsh village that storms may be coming. The boats return to the harbour heavy with their catch of the day, as a flock of shearwaters fly back to their nesting sites for the night.

Can you help the seabirds navigate their way home through the mackerel sky?

Finish

Start

< Start

Did you know?

Mackerel skies spread out and cover a large part of the sky. They are made of cirrus clouds.

In some countries, this cloud formation is named after a sheep's fleece, cobblestones or even buttermilk.

Cirrus clouds usually occur above 5,500 metres (18,000 feet).

Rain falls from all types of cloud but since cirrus clouds are so high up, the rain never reaches the ground.

In Latin, *cirrus* means 'lock of hair'.

Can you spot: • fish in a bucket
• a lifejacket • a nautical flag?

7

DESERTS IN BLOOM

The Atacama Desert in Chile stretches from the Andes mountain range to the Pacific Ocean. It covers over 1,500 square kilometres (600 square miles) of land and enjoys the challenge of being the driest desert in the world. Tourists visit the area all year round to go sandboarding down the dunes, float in the rare salty lagoons or gaze at the stars in the exceptionally clear night sky. But the desert is not a very easy place to live. Food and water are hard to find. Trees and flowers struggle. Then, every five to seven years, huge amounts of rain come and the flowers burst into life. In Chile, this is called the *desierto florido*, or 'desert in bloom'.

How does this phenomenon happen?

1 Flower seeds lie buried in the dry, cracked soil of the desert. They can wait for years, only flowering when the conditions are right.

2 Every few years, the Pacific Ocean off the coast of South America warms up due to weakening winds.

Equator

3 The warming ocean brings rain to the very dry Atacama Desert. In just one day, the desert receives seven times the usual annual rainfall.

4 The rain water brings life to the seeds and flowers, which bloom across the usually dry land.

Colours of the Desert Maze

Can you spot: ● a bird ● a lizard ● a butterfly?

10

In the Atacama Desert, a sudden heavy rainfall has nourished seeds that have been buried underground for years. The landscape bursts into life with a carpet of pinks, oranges, yellows and purples, but many are damaged by visitors who want to see this spectacle for themselves.

Can you find a clear path through the desert to the mountains beyond, without stepping on the flowers?

Start

Did you know?

The flowers that bloom are small and do not last for very long.

The types of flowers that bloom include red and yellow añañucas, blue and pink suspiros, white and blue malvillas and yellow cartuchos.

Wildlife such as birds and lizards benefit from eating the insects that visit the flowers.

Since the desert is usually so dry, the heavy rain can cause landslides that endanger local people and villages.

There is a desert in Utah, USA and another in Australia that also flower after high levels of rain.

SUPERCELLS

Big, dark rain clouds, thunder and lightning create dramatic scenes in our skies, called thunderstorms. This happens when warm, wet air rises, pushing a dense, vertical cloud – known as a cumulonimbus cloud – upward. Small bits of ice form in the rising cloud and crash together, sparking lightning bolts that make loud thunder claps. As the cloud rises, rain starts to fall, creating a downward draft of cool air. This cool, downward draft usually weakens the warm, upward draft, calming the storm. But sometimes the upward draft gets too strong and a supercell storm is created, which can lead to tornadoes.

How does this phenomenon happen?

1

Thunderstorms form from moist, rising, unstable air. For a supercell to form, a warm, upward draft of air also rotates and speeds up with height.

warm air

2 The rain produced by the storm creates a cooling downward draft but it is too far away from the upward draft to weaken it. The storm gets stronger and becomes a supercell.

warm air

cool air

3 Supercells usually produce light or heavy hail showers on top of the rain.

4 The rotating upwards draft can produce damaging wind and even small tornadoes.

A Supercell Storm

Start

In Tornado Alley in the United States, a powerful supercell storm is forming. Warm, moist air is flooding into the region and meeting with a strong upward draft of air to kick off a powerful rotating storm, spinning faster and faster as it rises. Then a dazzling lightning show streaks through the clouds, adding to the spectacle in the sky.

Can you find a path through this supercell all the way from the sky to the ground?

Can you spot: ● a pick-up truck ● a bird ● a storm-chaser?

Did you know?

These storms are extreme weather events that can cause a lot of damage.

Around one third of supercell storms create tornadoes.

The rotating upward draft in the storm is called a *mesocyclone*.

The upward draft creates an overshooting top that extends past the top of the storm cloud.

Most thunderstorms do not develop into supercell storms.

Finish

NORTHERN LIGHTS

There is a magical light show that appears in the sky around the North and South Poles. It is called *aurora*, which is a Latin word that means 'dawn'. People usually call it the Northern Lights but, officially, the lights are called *aurora borealis* in the Northern Hemisphere and *aurora australis* in the Southern Hemisphere. Aboriginal people in South Australia thought the lights were campfires started by spirits but scientists have discovered that it comes from particles carried in solar winds – 'winds of the Sun' – that make these moving curtains of multicoloured light bend, shift and change in front of our eyes.

How does this phenomenon happen?

1 Earth has a magnetic field surrounding it. The magnetic activity is particularly strong around the polar regions.

2 Particles from the Sun that are carried on solar winds penetrate Earth's magnetic shield and collide with molecules in our atmosphere. These collisions create bursts of light that make up the visible aurora.

3 Collisions between particles and different molecules make different coloured lights. As the particles are attracted most strongly to the poles, the aurora happens near the magnetic North or South Pole.

4 The solar winds that carry the particles can be very strong or very weak at different times. A solar storm will result in a huge display of the aurora.

Witnessing the Lights

Start

Finish

18

Did you know?

The French astronomer Pierre Gassendi came up with the name *aurora borealis* after witnessing them as far south as France.

'Aurora' is the name of a Roman god and means 'dawn'. 'Boreas' is the Greek god of the North Wind.

The light show can happen during the day, too, but it is not very visible.

Human eyes are limited in terms of what they can see of the auroras but cameras are sometimes able to pick up clearer images.

The Hubble Space Telescope shows light displays happening on Jupiter and Saturn, too.

The Inuit people of Alaska are preparing to feast on meat caught by the hunters of the group. In the lights of the *aurora borealis*, they are said to see the souls of animals that they have hunted.

Can you guide the hunters in their boats through the ice to dry land?

Can you spot: ● a polar bear hunting for food ● a caught fish ● an igloo?

BIOLUMINESCENT WAVES

Certain plants and creatures are bioluminescent. This means that they use luminescent proteins and fluorescent molecules in their bodies to glow in the dark. Being able to glow in this way is a very important skill. Aside from when fireflies and their larvae (glow-worms) put on a show in forests or caves, humans will rarely witness bioluminescence in the wild because it usually happens at the bottom of deep, dark oceans. But occasionally the ocean brings brightly lit plankton to the shore. There, they create a mesmerising display in the waves that lap the beaches.

How does this phenomenon happen?

1 Plankton is a collection of organisms, such as algae, that drift around in the oceans. A certain type of plankton – bioluminescent phytoplankton – is able to produce light using a chemical called *luciferin*.

2 The phytoplankton have developed this light-making ability as a way of surprising and disorientating predators. The phytoplankton glow whenever they are stressed – such as when they are moved or touched.

3 Sometimes, ocean currents stir up bioluminescent phytoplankton in the depths of the sea and bring them to the shore in vast numbers.

4 When a wave full of these bioluminescent phytoplankton crashes on the shore, or a surfboard skims past them, they become stressed and produce their distinctive glow.

Waves of Sea Sparkle

On the shores of San Diego in California, waves glow blue during a phytoplankton bloom. These phenomena are hard to predict, but when they do happen, surfers are quick to take to the waters, with their boards cutting a magical path through the bioluminescent sea. Footsteps in the sand sparkle like glitter, left behind by other witnesses of this spectacular event.

Can you find a trail through the magical plankton from the lighthouse to the shore?

Finish

< Start

Did you know?

Phytoplankton are a type of plant and a major food source for marine wildlife such as fish.

If a predator swallows bioluminescent plankton, the predator itself may begin to glow, attracting a secondary, larger predator towards it.

The light that bioluminescent phytoplankton emit is known as 'cold light'. This is because less than 20% of the light creates any heat.

Another name for these plankton is 'sea sparkle'.

Bioluminescent waves are seen around the world in countries such as Australia, Vietnam, Puerto Rico and Thailand.

Can you spot: ● a starfish ● a crab ● a pair of flip-flops?

WATERFALL RAINBOWS

Sunlight contains seven different colours: red, orange, yellow, green, blue, indigo and violet. Each colour moves like a wave and together the colours look white. When a ray of sunlight hits a drop of water at a certain angle our eyes can see the separate waves. This is called a rainbow. Since it is a visual effect, you cannot touch or get close to a rainbow – as it only moves further away from you. Other types of water droplet can also create a rainbow, such as the mist at the bottom of a very high waterfall. These rainbows appear in various shapes in the mist.

How does this phenomenon happen?

1 Some of the water pouring over the steep edge of a very tall waterfall turns to mist on the way down.

sunlight

2 Sunlight enters the water droplets and hits the back of the droplet before being reflected back out of the droplet again. When it exits the droplet, the light is bent and spreads out into a band of colours we know as a rainbow.

raindrop

rainbow

3 The angle at which the sunlight bounces back out of the droplet is very important as only certain angles create a rainbow. The best rainbows need a 42-degree angle.

4 We are now able to see these separate colour waves with our eyes. The mist at the bottom of the waterfall creates a glowing rainbow effect.

A Rainbow in the Mist

On a sunny day, rainbows can often be seen in the mist of Skógafoss waterfall in Iceland. Legend speaks of a treasure chest hidden behind the waterfall, put there by the first Viking settler in the area. Locals once laid hands on the handle of the chest before it disappeared in front of their eyes…

Can you help these treasure hunters find their way to the gold?

start

Finish

Did you know?

'Richard of York Gave Battle in Vain' helps you remember the order of the colours of the rainbow.

Angel Falls in Venezuela is the tallest waterfall in the world at 979 metres high (3,212 feet).

Because the light wave of red is the longest, it makes the biggest curve at the top and the other colours make smaller curves underneath.

Rainbows are usually a complete circle but we can only see the half above ground.

Some plastics or glass can catch light and project a rainbow onto a surface.

VOLCANIC ERUPTIONS

The Earth is round. At its centre – the core – nestles solid iron and nickel, surrounded by a layer of liquid iron and nickel. The next layer is called the mantle, which is very hot, almost-liquid rock that becomes more solid nearer the surface of the planet. All of this is enclosed by the Earth's crust, which is up to 60 kilometres (36 miles) thick. Where separate parts of the crust meet and push against each other, they form peaks, mountain ranges and volcanoes. In a volcano, when the conditions are right, the solid mantle melts into magma, which erupts as lava.

How does this phenomenon happen?

magma

upper crust

lower crust

1 Extreme heat in the Earth's crust causes parts of the rock to melt, forming a liquid rock called magma. When a large body of magma forms, it is known as a magma chamber.

the mantle

liquid iron and nickel

solid iron and nickel

2 As the magma cools, gases build up, creating pressure that can drive the magma towards the surface of the Earth. Movements in the Earth's plates can also cause such pressure.

3 Thin magma releases more gas and so the pressure is less than if the magma is thick. When the magma eventually erupts through the crust, the lava flows down the side of the volcano.

thin magma eruption

thick magma eruption

4 Thick magma keeps hold of gases, building up the pressure until it erupts much more violently. The lava from the eruption eventually cools to form a new crust.

A Volcanic Lava Flow

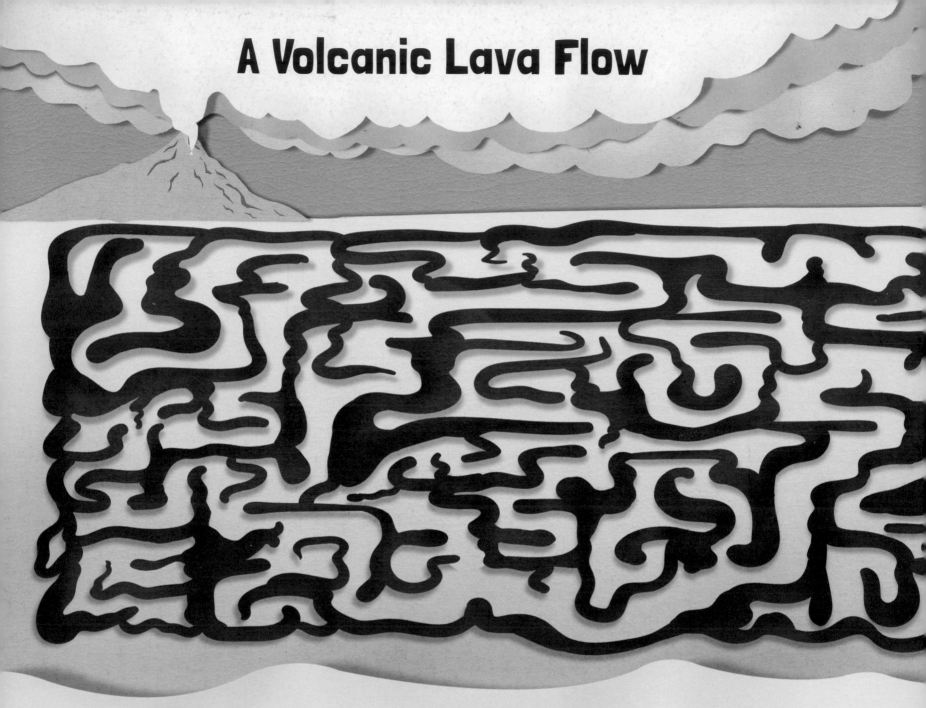

At the most active volcano in the world, Kilanea in Hawaii, the lava has carved out a path through the island landscape to the shore. People believe its crater is the home of the goddess of fire, lightning and volcanoes.

Can you find a clear route through the lava from the crater to the sea?

Start >

Finish

Did you know?

Volcanoes occur not only on land but on the ocean floor and under ice caps.

Over 75% of the world's most active volcanoes are found in the Pacific Ring of Fire – an area in the basin of the Pacific Ocean.

In 1883, a volcano on the Indonesian island of Krakatoa erupted with 13,000 times the power of an atomic bomb.

A volcano's eruption can send ash over 30 kilometres (17 miles) into the air.

Extremely large volcanic eruptions are capable of reflecting radiation from the Sun, causing the temperature on Earth to marginally drop.

Can you spot: ● a sea turtle ● a red bird ● a yellow bird?

Answers

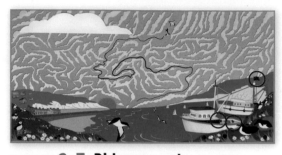

pages 6-7 **Did you spot:** ● fish in a bucket ● a lifejacket ● a nautical flag?

pages 8-9 **Did you spot:** ● a bird ● a lizard ● a butterfly?

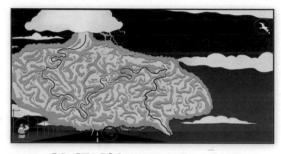

pages 14-15 **Did you spot:** ● a pick-up truck ● a bird ● a storm-chaser?

pages 18-19 **Did you spot:** ● a polar bear hunting for food ● a caught fish ● an igloo?

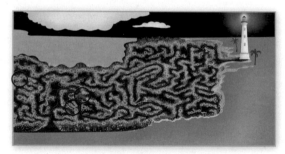

pages 22-23 **Did you spot:** ● a starfish ● a crab ● a pair of flip-flops?

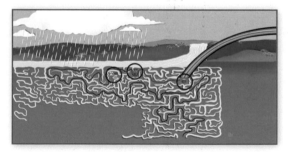

pages 26-27 **Did you spot:** ● a black sheep ● a pot of gold ● a photographer?

pages 30-31 **Did you spot:** ● a sea turtle ● a red bird ● a yellow bird?

Published by b small publishing ltd.
Text and illustrations © b small publishing ltd. 2018
1 2 3 4 5 6 7 8 9 10
British Library Cataloguing-in-Publication Data: A catalogue record for this book is available from the British Library.

ILLUSTRATIONS: Sarah Dennis **DESIGN:** Karen Hood **COVER DESIGN:** Vicky Barker
EDITORIAL: Eryl Nash & Jenny Jacoby **PRODUCTION:** Madeleine Ehm

Printed in China by WKT Co. Ltd. ISBN 978-1-911509-25-7
Please visit our website if you would like to contact us: www.bsmall.co.uk